COMPUTERS FOR KIDS

APPLE II PLUS EDITION

COMPUTERS FOR KIDS

APPLE II PLUS EDITION

SALLY GREENWOOD LARSEN

creative computing press

Copyright© 1981 by Creative Computing.

All rights reserved. No portion of this book may be reproduced—mechanically, electronically, or by any other means, including photocopying—without written permission of the publisher.

Library of Congress Number: 80-68961
ISBN: 0-9166 88-21-6

Printed in the United States of America.
First printing January 1981.

10 9 8 7 6 5 4 3 2 1

Creative Computing Press
P.O. Box 789-M
Morristown, NJ 07960

For my grandmother,
Irene Greenwood,
Who has always insisted
I get my "smarts" from
her side of the family.

Books From Creative Computing Press

If you cannot find Computers For Kids or other Creative Computing Press books locally, they can be ordered directly from the publisher. Add $2.00 shipping and handling per order. (Foreign orders add $2.00 for each book). NJ residents add 5% sales tax.

VISA, MasterCharge or American Express orders can be called in toll free: **800-631-8112** (In NJ 201-540-0445).

The Best of Creative Computing - Volume I — Ahl	$8.95
The Best of Creative Computing - Volume II — Ahl	8.95
The Best of Creative Computing - Volume III — Ahl & Green	8.95
The Best of Byte — Ahl & Helmers	11.95
Computers in Mathematics: A Sourcebook of Ideas — Ahl	15.95
Basic Computer Games — Ahl	7.50
More Basic Computer Games — Ahl & North	7.95
More Basic Computer Games - TRS-80 Edition — Ahl & North	7.95
Problems for Computer Solution — Rogowski	4.95
Problems for Computer Solution - Teacher's Edition — Rogowski	9.95
Computer Coin Games — Weisbecker	3.95
Computers For Kids — TRS-80, Apple or Atari Edition — Larsen	3.95
Be a Computer Literate — Ball & Charp	3.95
Katie and the Computer — D'Ignazio & Gilliam	6.95
The Impact of Computers on Society and Ethics : A Bibliography — Abshire	17.95
Tales of the Marvelous Machine: Thirty-five Stories of Computing — Taylor & Green	7.95
The Colossal Computer Cartoon Book — Ahl	4.95
Computer Music Festival Record	6.00
Computer Rage Game	8.95

Subscriptions to Creative Computing magazine are available for $20 for 12 issues; $37 for 24 issues; or $53 for 36 issues. For foreign surface add $9 per year. For foreign air mail add $30 per year.

creative computing

P.O. Box 789-M
Morristown, NJ 07960

TABLE OF CONTENTS

Section	page
1: What Is a Computer?	1
2: Flowcharting	4
3: Running the Computer Itself	9
4: Saving your Programs with a Cassette Recorder	13
5: Saving your Programs with a Disk Drive	17
6: Getting Ready to Program	22
7: PRINT and Variables	25
8: GOTO and INPUT	38
9: IF-THEN and FOR-NEXT	41
10: Graphics Programs	48
11: Sample Programs	56
12: Glossary of Statements and Commands	58
Notes for Parents and Teachers	64

SECTION 1: What is a Computer?

When a caveman had work to do, he had no machines or tools to help him. He had to do it all by himself. Man has since invented many tools to help him with his work.

Instead of pounding with his hands, he now uses a hammer. The hammer lets him pound harder and longer than he could pound with his hands alone.

Man invented the telescope so that he could see farther into space. He can now see stars he did not know existed before he had the telescope to help his eyes.

Using his brain, man can remember information and solve problems.

Man wanted to invent a tool so that he could extend the use of his brain, so he invented the COMPUTER.

Just as a hammer can't do work without a person to hold it, a computer cannot do work without a person to run it and tell it what to do. This person is called a PROGRAMMER.

Even the best hammer cannot do all the different things our hands can do. And even the best computer cannot do everything our brains can do.

A computer cannot feel emotion. It cannot feel happy or sad, as we can.

A computer cannot combine ideas the way our brain can. It can't put two ideas together and take the best parts of each one to make a brand new idea.

But . . . a computer **can** do some of the simpler jobs our brains can do. And it can do some of them even faster than we can!

A computer can remember many more things than most of us can with just our brains, especially things like long lists of names or numbers. This information is kept inside the computer in the MEMORY. Computer programmers call this information DATA.

A computer can **compare** data to see if one thing is bigger than another, or smaller, or the same. It can also put things in order.

A computer can sort many pieces of data and put together the things that are alike.

And a computer can look in its memory to find the data a programmer wants, and print out that data on a video screen or a sheet of paper.

This book is about the APPLE II PLUS microcomputer, made by APPLE Computer, Inc.

These are special directions for *this* computer. They will not work on all other kinds of computers.

The APPLE II PLUS is called a MICROCOMPUTER, because it is so small. Many businesses and universities have computers, too, but theirs have to do many more jobs than the APPLE II PLUS, so they have to be much larger. Some of the biggest computers are so huge, they fill an entire *room*!

The APPLE II PLUS uses a special computer language called BASIC. It is an easy language to learn, because it uses words we hear every day.

Some bigger computers use languages called FORTRAN or COBOL. You might hear about other languages when you find out more about computers.

SECTION 2: Flowcharting

When you want the computer to do a job for you, you must break down the job into small steps, so the computer can understand what to do. One big job may have many small steps, and sometimes it is hard to keep track of all the steps.

One way of keeping track is with a **flowchart**. A flowchart shows all the steps in a problem, shows what choices there are, and in what order the steps must be done.

On the next page is a flowchart showing all the little steps in a funny problem. The directions on this flowchart are things for you to do. They are not directions for the computer!

The shapes drawn around the steps show what **kind** of a step it is:

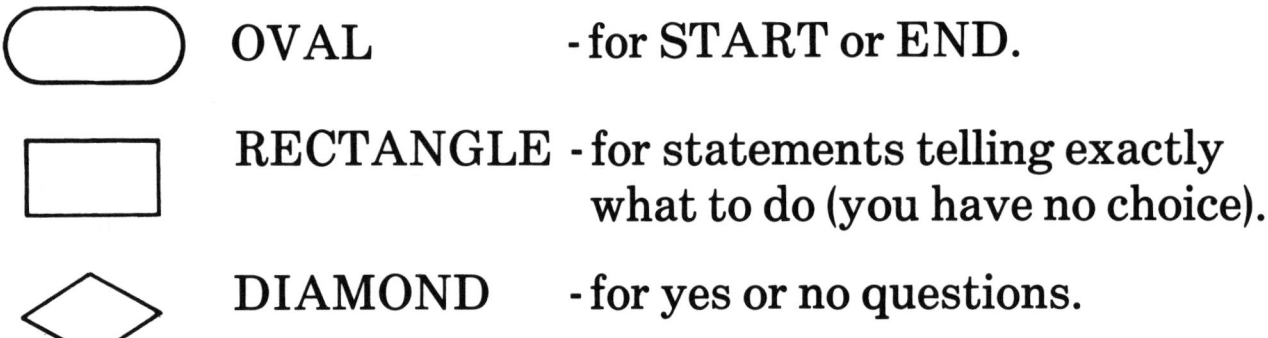

How to Scare Your Mom with an Elephant

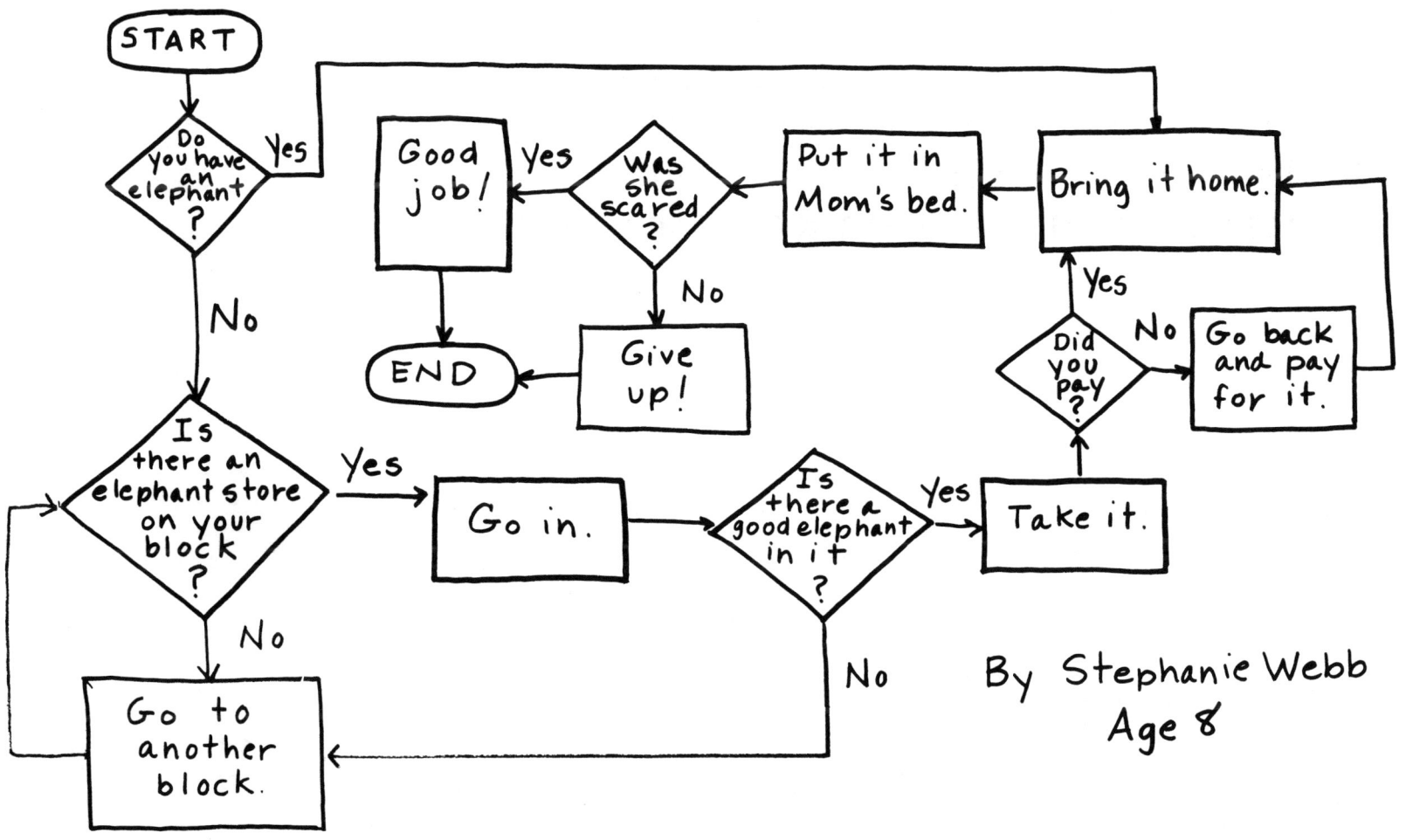

By Stephanie Webb
Age 8

The arrows on a flowchart show you what to do next. One arrow shows what to do if the answer is *yes*. The other arrow is for *no*.

There must be no "dead ends" in a flowchart. This means that there must always be an arrow showing what to do and where to go next.

Find the "dead end" in this little flowchart:

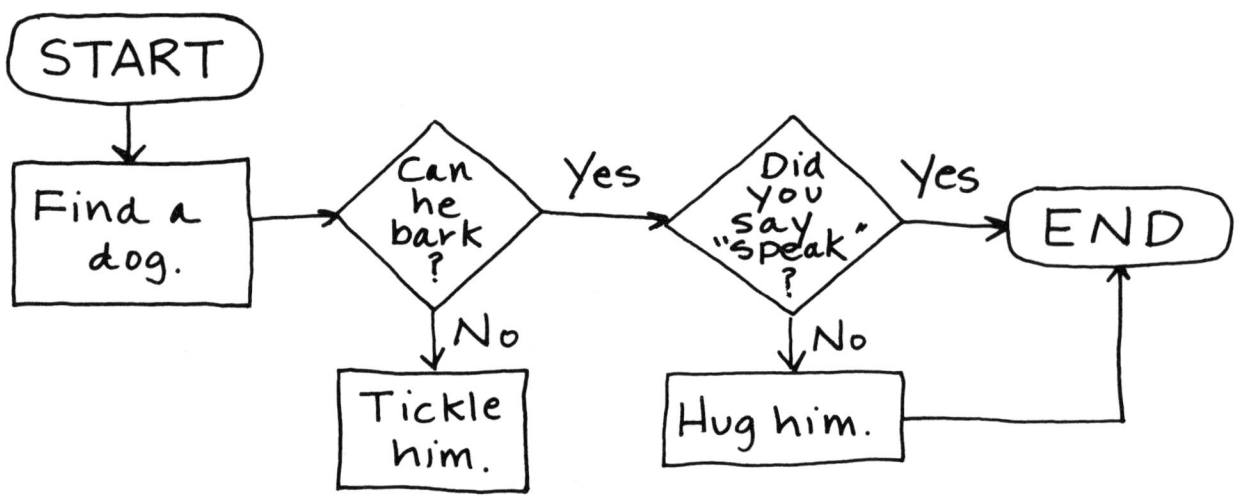

ANSWER: The dead end is tickle him . Once you get to that statement, there is no arrow showing you where to go next.

When you write your own practice flowcharts, pick a subject you know something about. Also, your flowchart will be much more interesting if you pick a topic which has some choices in it. You want both questions *and* statements in your flowchart—not just a page full of one statement after another. Here are some suggestions:

1. How to make a peanut butter and jelly sandwich.
2. How to take a bath.
3. How to make your mother scream.
4. How to play kickball.
5. How to buy a birthday present.

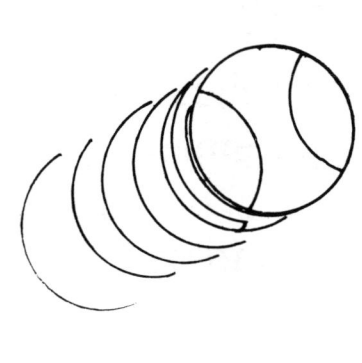

When the arrows in a flowchart make you do something over and over again, this is called a *DO-LOOP*. Here is an example: (I have only drawn *part* of this flowchart.)

How To Get A Date With Miss Piggy

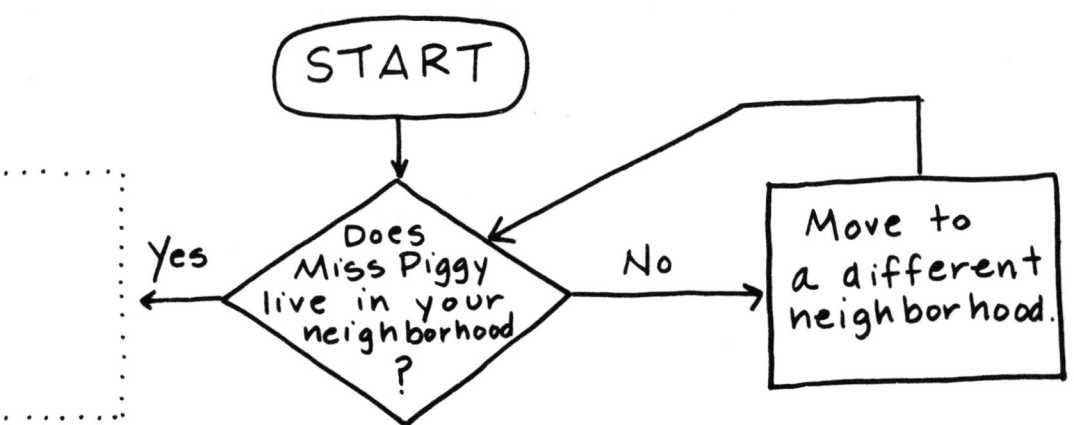

If you follow the directions for this part of the flowchart, you will keep moving to a new neighborhood until you are living in Miss Piggy's neighborhood. This is called a **do-loop**.

In a do-loop, you keep coming back to the question you asked until you finally get the answer you need so you can go on to the rest of the flowchart. In the example on this page, in order to "get a date with Miss Piggy", you had to first move into her neighborhood.

In Section 8, you will see how we use flowcharts to help us write computer programs.

SECTION 3: Running the Computer Itself

The Apple II PLUS Computer has two basic parts:

The Keyboard - This looks like a regular typewriter keyboard. It has all the electronics for the computer inside it. You type in information and instructions for the computer on the keyboard.

The TV screen - The information you type on the keyboard is printed out on the TV screen, so you can see what you are doing. The keyboard can be hooked up to almost any TV set. However, when you learn to make pictures on the screen, you will see that you need a color TV to make colored pictures. (If you use a black and white TV, the pictures you make will be black and white.)

The computer has a *Random Access Memory* (RAM for short). This means that the computer will hold data in its memory only as long as the keyboard is left **on**, so it has electricity flowing through it. If you turn off or unplug the keyboard, you will lose your program. (Turning off only the TV won't matter.)

After you have written a program, you will want to be able to **save** that program some way, so the next time you want to use it, you won't have to type in the whole program again.

The APPLE II PLUS has two ways to **save** your programs—with a cassette tape recorder, or with a disk drive. Your computer will probably have either a recorder **or** a disk drive, and possibly both.

The cassette tape recorder is the same kind you use to record music. It is hooked to the keyboard with special wires.

The disk drive is a small square box, attached to the keyboard with a rainbow-colored "ribbon" of wires.

When you have written a program you want to save, you can find the directions for using the cassette recorder in Section 4, and the directions for the disk drive in Section 5.

The first time you use the APPLE II PLUS, have an adult help you set up the machine and connect all the proper plugs. It is not hard to set up the computer, once you know how, but it is important that the job be done correctly, or you will ruin it.

IF YOU AREN'T SURE—ASK FOR HELP!!! It could take weeks to get your computer fixed if you break it.

Things To Remember

1. Before you start programming, you must turn on both the TV and the keyboard. (If this doesn't work, you probably forgot to plug them into the wall socket.) The TV volume should be turned all the way down, so you can't hear any sounds from the TV.

2. Take it easy with the keyboard—no pounding, please!

3. Keep your feet away from the electrical cords. If you accidentally kick out a plug, you may lose your program.

4. Good programmers never eat or drink while working. The computer will not work well if it is full of cookie crumbs, or has soda spilled between the keys!

5. You should **never** remove the lid of the keyboard without an adult there to help you. If you reach inside and touch the wrong things, you could ruin your computer, or get an electrical shock. With the lid closed, your computer is as safe as any other appliance you have at home.

6. Turn off both the TV and the keyboard when you are not using them.

Unless you need to save a program right away, skip Sections 4 and 5 about the cassette recorder and the disk drive, and go right to Section 6—Getting Ready to Program.

You can come back to Sections 4 and 5 when you need them.

SECTION 4: Saving Your Programs with a Cassette Recorder

You now have a computer program typed into the computer, and you want to save it on a cassette tape. Follow these directions **carefully**.

Saving Your Program on a Cassette

1. Advance your cassette tape to the spot where you want to record your program. REMEMBER THE NUMBER ON THE TAPE RECORDER COUNTER! Just to be safe, make sure you have gone five numbers past the end of the last program on that tape.
2. Press down both the (PLAY) and (RECORD) buttons on the tape recorder. Hold them down until they stay.

3. Type SAVE on the computer and press the RETURN key.

4. The Cursor [■ will disappear from the screen while the program is being saved on your tape. The computer will "Beep" once when the recording begins. When the recording is finished, you will hear another "Beep", and the cursor will come back *on* the screen.

If the computer screen says
> SYNTAX ERROR

instead, the volume or tone setting on your cassette recorder is not right. Press RESET, adjust the volume (or tone), rewind the tape, and try again.

5. Turn off the tape recorder.

6. Your program is now recorded on the cassette. Make sure the location and subject of your program is written down on the cassette label, so you can find it later. Saving the program on a tape does not erase it from the computer's memory. You must type NEW to do that.

Special Notes:
* To be sure you get a good recording of an important program, you should record the program several times on the tape, with a little space between recordings, of course.

* You must use a good quality cassette tape, and it should be **new**. You should not record one program over the top of another, or erase an old music tape and use it for computer programs. Computer companies sell special short cassette tapes just for this use. They cost less than most tapes, and they work very well. You can save lots of programs on one short tape.

If you have saved a program on a cassette, and now want to load it into your computer, follow these directions carefully:

Loading a Cassette Tape Program into the Computer

1. Advance your cassette to two or three numbers **before** the location of your program. (If your program is recorded at 85, for example, advance the tape to 82 or 83 on the counter.)

2. Type LOAD on the computer. Do not press RETURN yet.

3. Press down the (PLAY) button on the tape recorder.

4. Press the RETURN key.

5. The cursor [■ will disappear from the screen while your program is being loaded into the memory. You will hear a "Beep" when the loading starts. When it is finished, you will hear another "Beep," and the cursor will appear again.

If the computer screen says
SYNTAX ERROR
instead, the volume or tone setting on your cassette recorder is not right. Press RESET , adjust the volume (or tone), rewind the tape, and try again.

6. Turn off the tape recorder.

7. Your program should now be in the memory of the computer. You can LIST it, or RUN it, just like any other program.

SECTION 5: Saving Your Programs with a Disk Drive

If you have a disk drive with your computer, you will be saving your programs on a round piece of magnetic material called a **floppy diskette**. In this book we will call it a **diskette**, for short.

Before you save a program on a diskette, you must give your program a name, like JOHN'S PROGRAM, or WORM RACE. The name will go right on the diskette with the program.

After you practice once or twice, you will find that using a disk drive is *very* easy.

If you have a program typed in on the computer and are ready to save it on a diskette, read these directions carefully.

IMPORTANT! Read the Special Notes at the end of this section before you use your disk drive the first time, or you may ruin it.

Saving Your Program on a Diskette

1. Choose a name for your program. It is easier if you pick a short name such as

    SURPRISE

2. Type SAVE SURPRISE (the name of your program) and press the RETURN key.

3. The red light on the front of the disc drive will come on, and you will hear little noises coming from inside. When the red light goes off, your program SURPRISE is saved on the diskette. Saving a program on the diskette does not erase it from the computer's memory. You must type NEW to do that.

4. You can check to see if the program is really on the diskette by typing CATALOG and pressing the RETURN key. This will turn on the disk drive and make the computer print a list of all the programs stored on that diskette. Before each program name you will see a number. This is a special code to show how much room the program needed. You won't need to use these numbers at all.

Now, suppose you want to find a certain program on a diskette and load it into the computer, so you can use it.

Loading a Diskette Program into the Computer

1. Type CATALOG and press the [RETURN] key. The disk drive light will come on, and the computer will print out a list of all the programs on that diskette.

2. Find the name of the program you want. Look carefully at how it is spelled.

3. Type LOAD SURPRISE if you want to load the program named SURPRISE into the computer. The name of the program must be spelled (and spaced) **exactly** the same as it is on the diskette catalog list, or the computer will print
   FILE NOT FOUND
   which means there is no program by that exact name on the diskette. (You will have to try again.)

4. The red light on the front of the disk drive will come on while SURPRISE is being loaded, and you will hear little noises inside the disk drive. The light will go off when the program is loaded.

5. The program you wanted is now in the computer's memory. You can use it the same way you would use any other program you typed in yourself.

If you decide you don't want a program on a diskette any longer, here is how to erase it:

Deleting (Erasing) a Program From a Diskette

1. Type DELETE JOHN'S SPECIAL PROGRAM and press the RETURN key. This will erase the program named JOHN'S SPECIAL PROGRAM from the diskette.

2. Type CATALOG and RETURN to be sure that JOHN'S SPECIAL PROGRAM is no longer listed for that diskette.

Special Notes
* You should **always** keep a diskette inside the disk drive. If you turn on the computer while the disk drive is empty, it will go around and around, looking for a program to load. This can damage your disk drive.

* Have an adult show you which way to put the diskette into the disk drive. Be careful not to do it upside down or backwards!

* Your diskettes should be kept in their special paper jackets, and should never be left out to get dirty, or be stepped on.

* Static electricity from your fingers or a diskette can ruin your disk drive. Especially in the wintertime, or if you are walking over rugs, your body will pick up a static electricity charge. Then if you reach over to put a diskette into the disk drive, that spark will jump from the diskette into the disk drive, which will damage the disk drive.

You can easily get rid of the static charge on your body by touching the metal plate on the power pack of the computer. (You can see this metal plate around the ON-OFF switch on the back of the computer.) Touching this plate is called "grounding yourself out." You must get into the habit of **always** doing this before you touch the disk drive.

SECTION 6: Getting Ready To Program

When you write a program, you are writing a list of instructions the computer needs to do a particular job, such as printing your name on the screen. These instructions are called **program statements**, and you'll learn more about them in Section 7.

But sometimes you need to tell the machine itself to do something, such as get rid of an old program so you can write a new one, or clear all the printing off the TV screen. These are called **commands**, because they are not part of a program. You type them in and press RETURN , and the computer does them right away.

(I wrote RETURN in a box, because it has a special key all its own on the keyboard, like CTRL and RESET .)

Program statements all have **line numbers** in front of them, to tell the computer which statement should be done first. (You will see these line numbers in Section 7.) Remember that commands do not have a line number because they are not part of a program.

Here are some of the **commands** you will need. Remember to press RETURN after each one you use.

HOME this clears all the printing off the screen, but it does *not* take your program out of the memory. Remember—just because the information isn't printed on the TV screen doesn't mean it isn't stored inside the computer any more!

NEW this erases your last program from the memory so you can start on a new program with a "clean" memory.

LIST this prints out, in order, whatever program statements you have typed into the memory so far.

CTRL-S by pushing the CTRL key and S at the same time, you can control how fast the computer will LIST a very long program that won't fit on the screen all at the same time. Press CTRL — S and the computer will *stop* listing the program. Press CTRL — S again, and it will continue with the list. You can start and stop as often as you like, by using CTRL — S each time.

RUN   this tells the computer you have finished typing in all the instructions in your program, and now you want the computer to do that job. This is called **executing** the program. When the computer is finished executing the program, it will print]■ on the screen. This is called the **cursor**, and it will blink off and on to show where you will be typing next.

CTRL -C   If the computer is in the middle of executing your program and you want it to stop, press CTRL and C at the same time. The computer will print

BREAK IN 10

which means that line 10 is the last line the computer worked on before you made it stop. For example, if the computer program was stopped at line 45, the computer would print

BREAK IN 45

CONT   If you change your mind and want the computer to continue executing the program after you pushed CTRL — C , type in CONT and press RETURN . The computer will continue at the place it had stopped.

SECTION 7: PRINT and Variables

Let's begin by writing a program using the PRINT statement.

We want to tell the computer that this program will be using the TV screen to print letters or numbers (rather than drawing pictures), so our first statement should be

```
5  TEXT
```

The TEXT statement lets us write on the whole screen, if we need it.

Now we'll use a PRINT statement to print out the following message:

```
5  TEXT
10 PRINT "HELLO!  I AM THE APPLE II PLUS!"
15 PRINT "THIS MUST BE YOUR FIRST PROGRAM."
20 END
```

... and the last line in the program will be an END statement to show the computer where the program ends.

Now—when we type in RUN and press the RETURN key, this is what the computer will show on the screen:

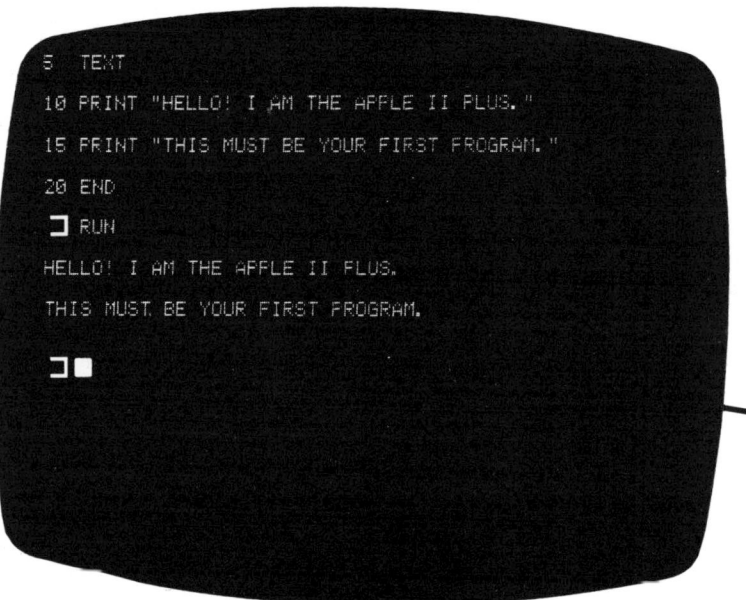

You try typing it in. Remember to press RETURN each time you finish typing a line.
RUN does not have a line number in front of it.

This is how the computer will follow the directions you gave it in your program.

When the computing is done following your instructions, this little blinking square (called a **cursor**) will appear, which shows that you are ready to type again.

Suppose you want the computer to run the same kind of program, but this time you want the instructions erased from the screen before the program is executed. In other words, you want the computer to erase the screen first, before it follows your instructions. Then when you RUN your program, the screen would look like this:

```
HELLO! I AM THE APPLE II PLUS.
THIS MUST BE YOUR FIRST PROGRAM.
```

To do this, all you need is one more statement in your program.

HOME

is a statement which tells the computer to erase the screen. Here's where it should go in your program:

```
5   TEXT
10  HOME
15  PRINT "HELLO!  I AM THE APPLE II PLUS."
20  PRINT "THIS MUST BE YOUR FIRST PROGRAM."
25  END
```

HOME is a very handy statement to remember. It helps you get any "garbage" off the screen that might be in the way when you run your program.

(You can also use HOME as a command, without a line number, just by typing HOME and pressing RETURN. You will use HOME and LIST often, when you write long programs of your own.)

Whenever you use a statement like PRINT "HELLO" the computer will print out **exactly** what you put between the quotation marks. Even if what you put is silly! Even if it's spelled incorrectly!

Here are some examples for you to try. Go ahead and make up some of your own!

```
5  TEXT
10 HOME
15 PRINT "I KIN SPELL REEL GOOD."
20 PRINT "GIGGLE!  GIGGLE!"
25 END
RUN
```

(RUN is *not* part of the program, but I'm putting it here so you don't forget to type it in every time you want to *run* your program. Later, I won't write it down each time.)

```
10 TEXT                                5  TEXT
20 HOME                                10 HOME
30 PRINT "MY NAME IS JOHN SMITH."      15 PRINT "I AM A FRIENDLY COMPUTER"
40 PRINT "MY NAME IS MARY JONES."      20 END
50 END                                 RUN
RUN
```

Before we go on with PRINT statements, let's talk about **line numbers**.

Every statement in a program has a number in front of it. This tells the computer which statement to do first. The computer will start with the lowest number and end with the highest number, no matter how many numbers you skip in between. Good programmers always count by 5's or 10's when they number their lines, so that if they leave out a line by mistake, they can put it in later, and there will be room. For example:

```
5  TEXT
10 HOME
15 PRINT "MY NAME IS ROBBIE."
20 PRINT "MY BIRTHDAY IS JULY 3RD."
25 END
```

Now—if I wanted to put a line in my program telling how old Robbie is, right after line 15, I could just type in:

```
18 PRINT " I AM 9 YEARS OLD."
```

If I type in HOME to clear the screen, then type LIST, the computer will put line 18 into the program, in the right place, and this is how the program will appear:

```
5   TEXT
10  HOME
15  PRINT "MY NAME IS ROBBIE."
18  PRINT "I AM 9 YEARS OLD."
20  PRINT "MY BIRTHDAY IS JULY 3RD."
25  END
```

This is very helpful if you forget something in your program.

You can use the same idea to **delete** (take out) a line in your program, if you make a mistake or just decide you don't want that line anymore.

```
5  TEXT
10 HOME
15 PRINT "TODAY IS TOOSDAY."
20 END
```

In this program, line 15 has a spelling mistake. To get rid of line 15 completely, all you do is type in:

```
15
```

and hit the return key. This will erase line 15 from the memory, and you can type in a new line 15.

But, suppose you are typing a line and you notice right away that you've made a mistake, even before you go on to the next line. Can you erase part of a line? OF, COURSE! All you do is press the ⬅ key until you move the cursor on top of the mistake. Now you can type in the correct letters.

Remember that the ⬅ key only works for the line you are typing on right then. If you are typing on line 15, you cannot erase something on line 5 with the ⬅ key. You will have to type in a whole new line 5.

You may also be wondering why zero is written with a line through it, like this:

$$\emptyset$$

This is done on computers so that there is no mix-up between the number zero and the letter O. You should use the special zero when you write your programs on paper, too.

When you type in commands or run your own programs on the APPLE II PLUS, if you type in something the computer does not understand, it may print

SYNTAX ERROR

on the screen. This means that you have made a spelling mistake in a statement or command, or you have used the wrong statement. These messages from the computer are called **error messages**. They help you figure out what kind of mistake you have made, so you can fix it.

This computer has several different error messages, for different kinds of mistakes. The one you will see most often is

SYNTAX ERROR

The PRINT statement can also be used to skip a line.

```
5   TEXT
10  HOME
15  PRINT "HELLO"
20  PRINT
25  PRINT "GOOD-BYE"
30  END
```

Without the quotation marks in a PRINT statement, the APPLE II PLUS will work like a calculator:

```
5   TEXT
10  HOME
15  PRINT 10 + 20
20  END
```

This program will print out the **answer** to 10 + 20, which is 30. If you wanted the computer to print out the actual problem of 10 + 20, you would write it like this:

```
10 PRINT "10 + 20"
```

Notice the difference?

Here is a PRINT program and the results on the screen when the program is executed. Look it over carefully.

```
5   TEXT
10  HOME
15  PRINT "RED"
20  PRINT "     BLUE"
25  PRINT "YELLOW"
30  PRINT "5 + 6"
35  PRINT 5 + 6
40  PRINT
45  PRINT "PINK PICKLES"
50  END
```

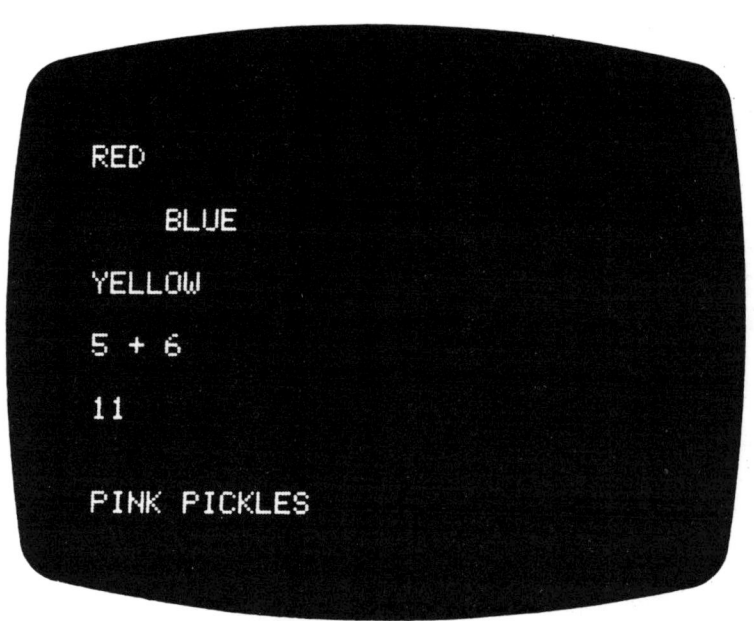

Notice that line 50 END does **not** print the word "END" on the screen. It just tells the computer that this is the **end** of your program.

The computer can also keep a number in its memory, and print it out later when you ask for it. Let's look at how the memory works.

The memory is like a big Post Office, with letters of the alphabet on each "mailbox." You put a number in a "mailbox" by using a LET statement.

```
45 LET A=5
50 LET B=7
55 LET C=2
60 LET D=0
```

A	B	C	D
5	7	2	0

Now whenever you use this statement in your program,

```
70 PRINT A
```

the computer will print out the number or **value** in the mailbox called "A". Of course, if you want the computer to print out the value of "A," you must make sure you put a number in mailbox "A" earlier in your program, or the computer will assume you wanted the value in mailbox "A" to be *zero*. This works for all the memory locations. If you do not put a number in a memory location, the computer will assume the value is zero.

In computer programs, the letter names you give to the "mailboxes" are called *variables*.

If you write a statement like

```
10 PRINT A+B
```

the computer will look in "A" to see what the value is, then find the value for *B*, and add them together and print out just the answer for you. Here is an example:

```
5  TEXT
15 HOME
25 LET A=6
35 LET B=4
45 PRINT A+B
55 END
```

Later in your program, if you want to change the number stored in mailbox A, you can use another LET statement. This will erase the old value for "A" and put in the new one.

The APPLE II PLUS uses a few special symbols for arithmetic:

Addition +	3 plus 4 is written as 3 + 4
Subtraction −	5 minus 2 is written as 5 − 2
Multiplication *	6 times 8 is written as 6*8
Division /	6 divided by 2 is written as 6/2

You can use the computer in the **command mode** to do math problems for you.

The **command mode** means that the computer executes each line as soon as you press the RETURN key. You are using the command mode when you type in NEW or LIST or RUN when you write programs.

PRINT can also be used the same way:

notice—no line number!

The answer to the problem will be printed on the screen as soon as you press RETURN.

SECTION 8: GOTO and INPUT

PRINT statements alone don't make very exciting programs. This section has two new statements which make programming more fun!

Let's look at each one, then write some simple programs.

GOTO tells the computer to *go to* the line number listed, and do what it says there.

```
5   TEXT
10  PRINT "HELLO"
15  GOTO 10
20  END
```

Every time the computer gets to line 15, the program tells it to go to line 10.

This program prints "HELLO" over and over and over again. The computer would print HELLO all night long, if you forgot to turn it off! Remember, you can stop the program with Control-C.

HELLO
HELLO
HELLO
HELLO
HELLO

INPUT asks you to type in a number while the program is running.

```
 5 TEXT
15 HOME
25 PRINT "TYPE IN YOUR AGE."
35 INPUT A
```

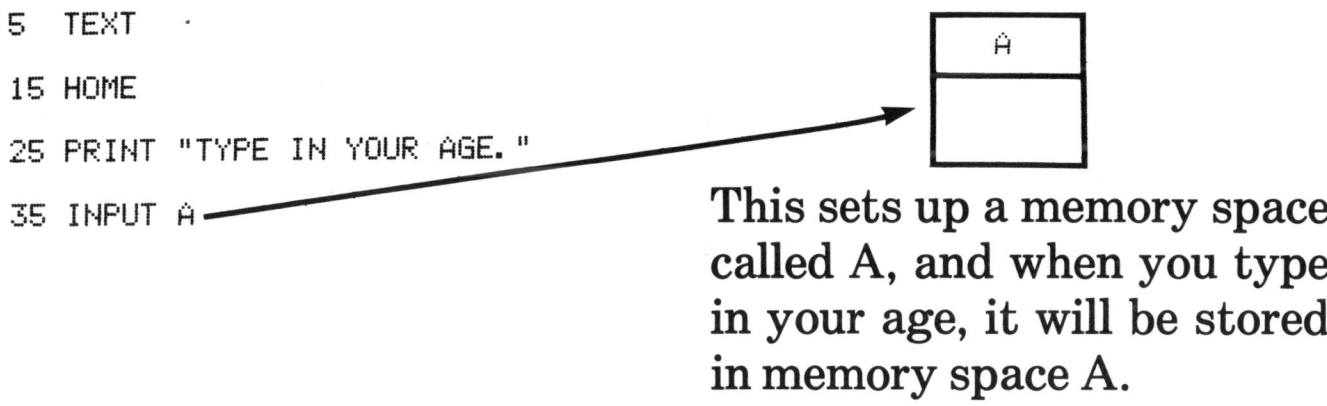

This sets up a memory space called A, and when you type in your age, it will be stored in memory space A.

Now we can use that information:

```
45 PRINT "YOUR AGE IS"
55 PRINT A
65 END
```

This line will print out the number stored in memory space "A".

Type this program on the computer and try it yourself. You will notice that when the computer reaches an INPUT statement when it is running a program, it will print "?" and stop until you type in an answer. When you write your own INPUT programs, you must always be careful to put a statement before the INPUT telling the person who uses your program **what** the computer is waiting for them to type in.

Sometimes you want to stop using a program with an INPUT statement in it, but you can't, because the computer keeps printing

? REENTER

no matter what you type in. To get the program to stop, type CTRL — C and then RETURN . Now you can LIST your program and fix the mistakes, or type NEW and write another program.

SECTION 9: IF-THEN and FOR-NEXT

FOR-NEXT statements are *lots* of fun, because you can make the computer do all kinds of work for you!

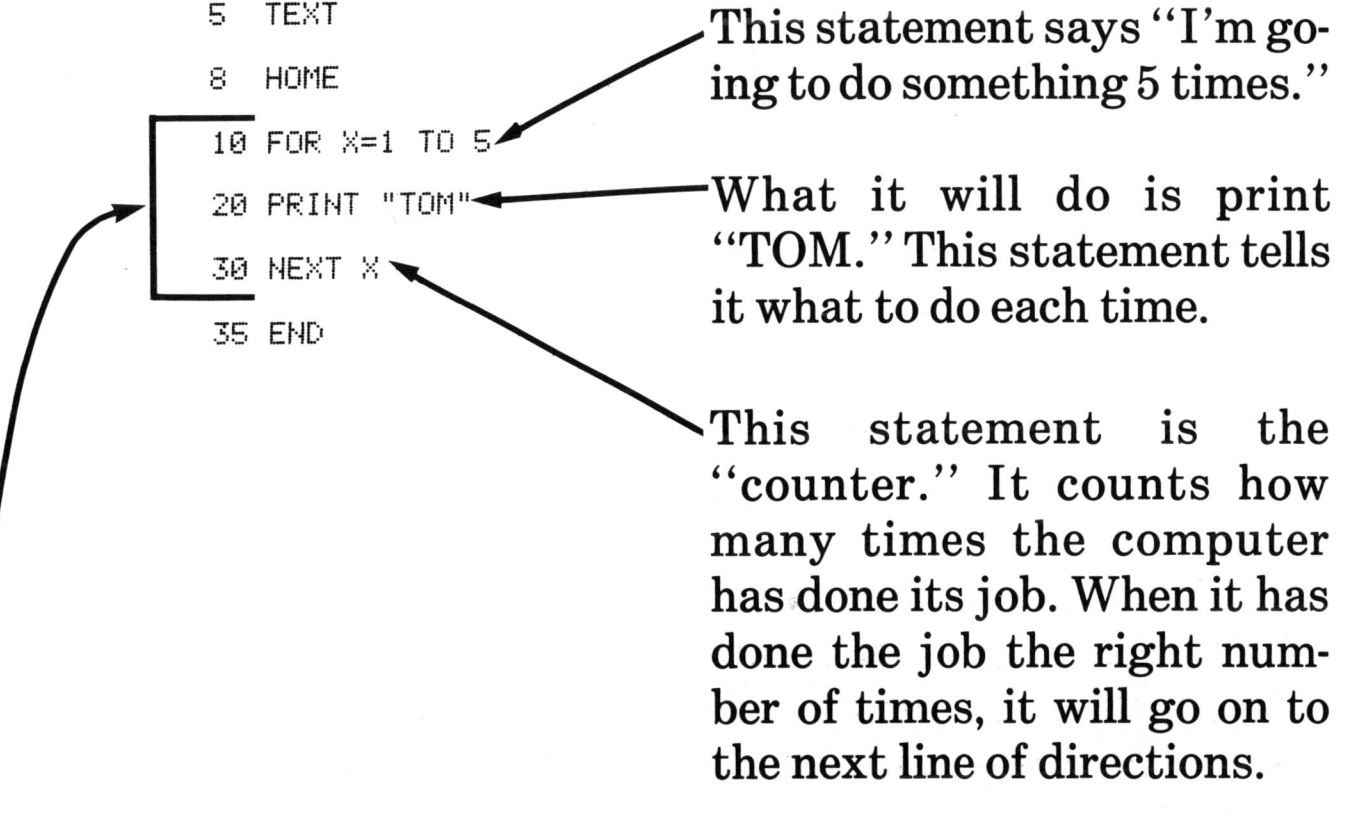

```
5  TEXT
8  HOME
10 FOR X=1 TO 5
20 PRINT "TOM"
30 NEXT X
35 END
```

This statement says "I'm going to do something 5 times."

What it will do is print "TOM." This statement tells it what to do each time.

This statement is the "counter." It counts how many times the computer has done its job. When it has done the job the right number of times, it will go on to the next line of directions.

This part of the program is called a **FOR-NEXT LOOP**, because the computer "loops" through that part of the program over and over again, until it has done its job the right number of times.

We can also write a program which has several lines between the FOR and NEXT statements in the loop:

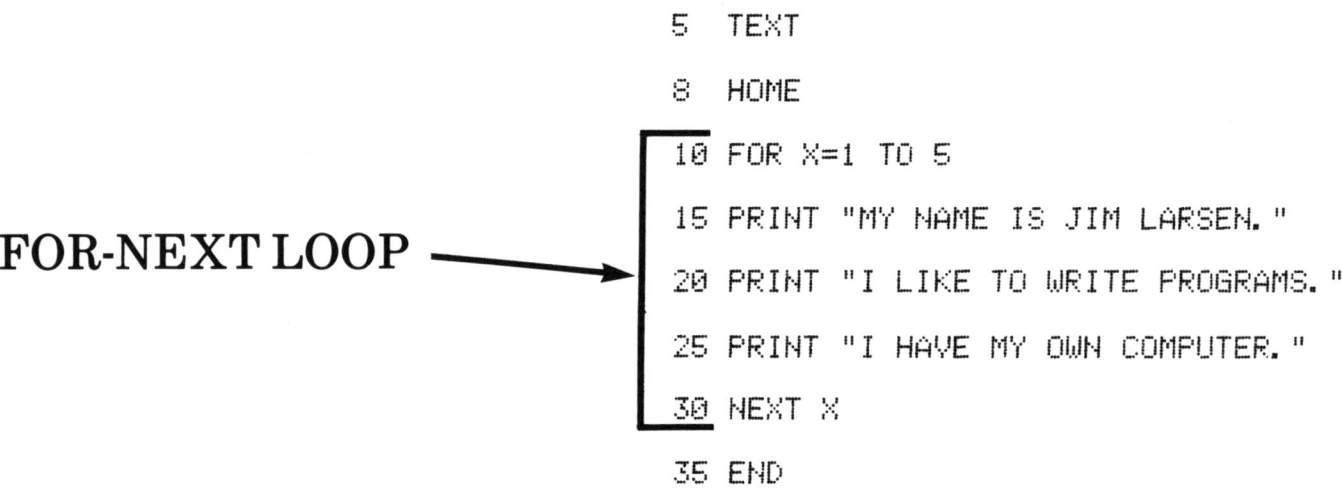

This program will write all three of the PRINT statements each time, until it has gone through the loop five times. It will print a total of 15 lines.

You may use any variable you wish in a FOR-NEXT loop, but the variable must be the *same* in both statements, or the computer will give you the error message NEXT WITHOUT FOR.

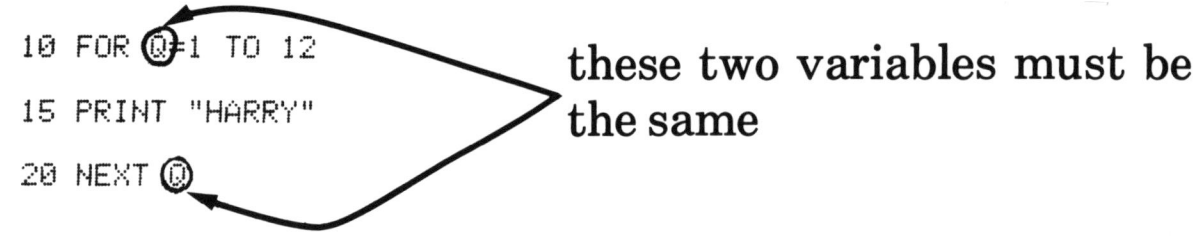

This program will print "HARRY" 12 times.

Let's look at how the counter works in a FOR-NEXT program.

```
10 FOR Q=1 TO 4
15 PRINT "I LOVE COMPUTERS."
20 NEXT Q
```

This statement sets up a memory space named Q. It tells the computer that the **values** stored in Q will start with 1 and end with 4.

```
10 FOR Q=1 TO 4
15 PRINT "HELLO"
```

Each time the computer goes through the FOR-NEXT loop one time (and prints "HELLO"), the value of Q is increased by one.

After doing line 15 PRINT "HELLO" the first time, the number stored in Q is 1.

Q
1

Q
2

Now the computer goes back to line 10 to start the loop again. After it prints line 15 and gets to

```
20 NEXT Q
```

the number in Q is increased by 1. (that's what NEXT Q means.)

43

This goes on until Q finally gets up to 4. Since the FOR-NEXT loop says

```
FOR Q=1 TO 4
```

the computer knows that once Q gets to 4, the FOR-NEXT loop is finished, and the computer should go on to the next statement in the program.

Here are a few sample problems to try. Now take some time and write your own!

NAME

```
5   TEXT
8   HOME
10  FOR Z=1 TO 100
15  PRINT "SUSAN IS GREAT"
20  NEXT Z
30  END
```

NUMBERS

```
5   TEXT
8   HOME
10  FOR R=1 TO 100
15  PRINT R
20  NEXT R
25  END
```

(In this program, you can see when the value of "R" changes!)

I have given these programs names, to make them easier to remember. Don't type in the name as part of the program, or the computer will give you an error message. (Of course, if you have a disk drive, you could use these names when you save the programs on a diskette.)

IF-THEN statements provide a "test" for your programs.

```
10 TEXT
20 HOME
30 PRINT "TYPE IN YOUR FAVORITE NUMBER."
40 INPUT N
50 IF N=5 THEN PRINT "YOU HAVE PICKED THE LUCKY NUMBER!"
60 END
```

This statement looks in "mailbox" N to see what number is stored there in the memory. If it is 5, then the computer is told to PRINT "You have picked the lucky number!" If the number is *not* 5 (if the number "fails" the test), then the computer ignores the rest of the statement and goes on to the next line.

Let's think about how IF-THEN statements work.

Pretend you are "inside" your program, and you are following all the instructions in the program, just as the computer would.

You are going down the road, and you come to a fork, where there are two ways to go.

This is the IF-THEN statement in the program you are following. Mr. IF has a "test" for you. If you pass the test, you may go down the fork in the road marked "THEN." If you do not pass the test, you must go the other way.

An IF-THEN statement is called a **branch** in your program.

We can also show this with a flowchart.

```
10 TEXT
20 HOME
30 PRINT "TYPE IN YOUR FAVORITE NUMBER."
40 INPUT N
50 IF N=5 THEN PRINT "YOU PICKED THE LUCKY NUMBER!"
60 END
```

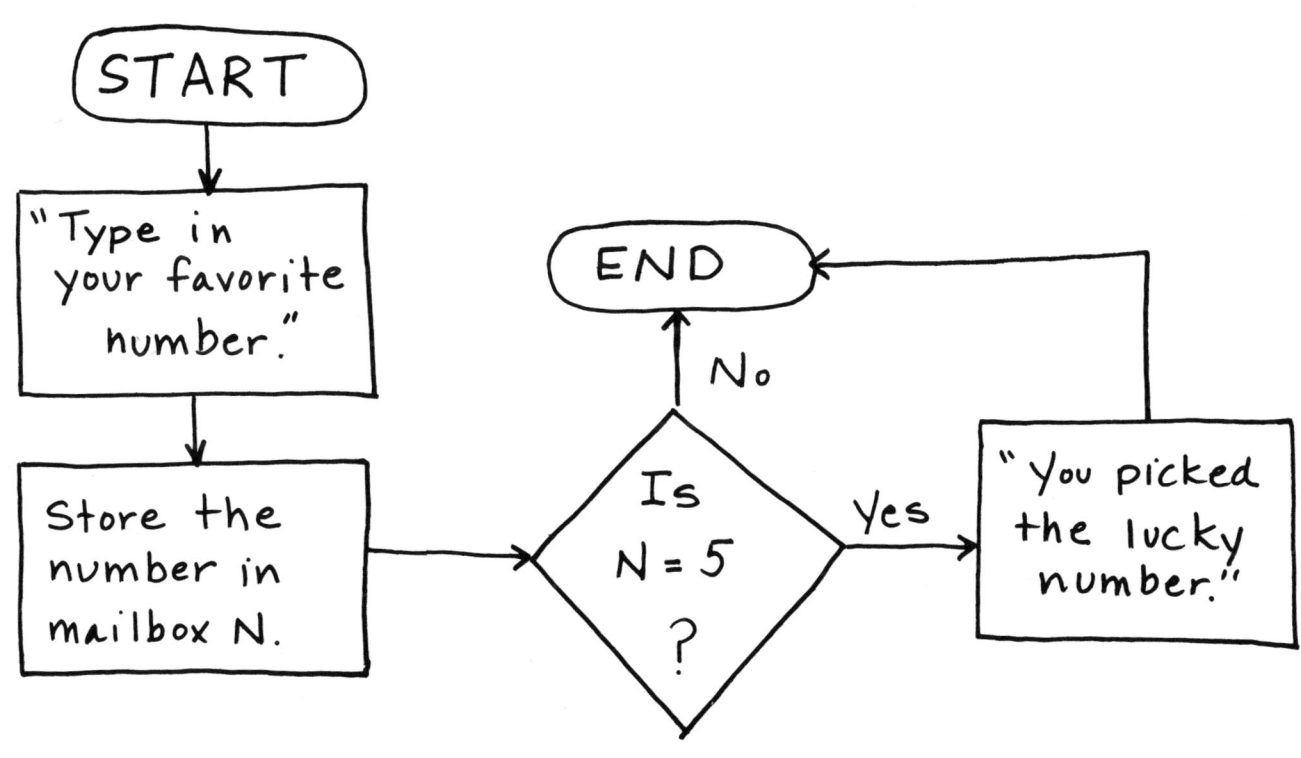

SECTION 10: Graphics Programs

Graphics programs let you make pictures on the TV screen with dots of light. Each dot (really a tiny square) has an address of its own. Your graphics program tells the computer which squares you want lighted.

The APPLE II PLUS is a special computer, because it has **color** graphics. Not only can you pick which squares you want, but you have 16 different colors to pick from!
Every graphics program must begin with the statement

```
5 GR
```

to tell the computer that you will be using almost all of the TV screen to make a picture. Only four lines on the very bottom of the screen can be used for letters or numbers, in a graphics program.

Before you tell the computer which squares you want to light up, you have to pick a color.

Each color has its own number. The color statement in your program looks like this:

`10 COLOR=13` ←—**This picks the color yellow**

Here are the colors and their numbers.

0 Black	8 Brown
1 Magenta	9 Orange
2 Dark Blue	10 Gray (a little different from 5)
3 Purple	11 Pink
4 Dark Green	12 Green
5 Gray	13 Yellow
6 Medium Blue	14 Aqua
7 Light Blue	15 White

The graphics screen is divided up into 40 squares across and 40 squares down. (Part of the screen is shown here.)

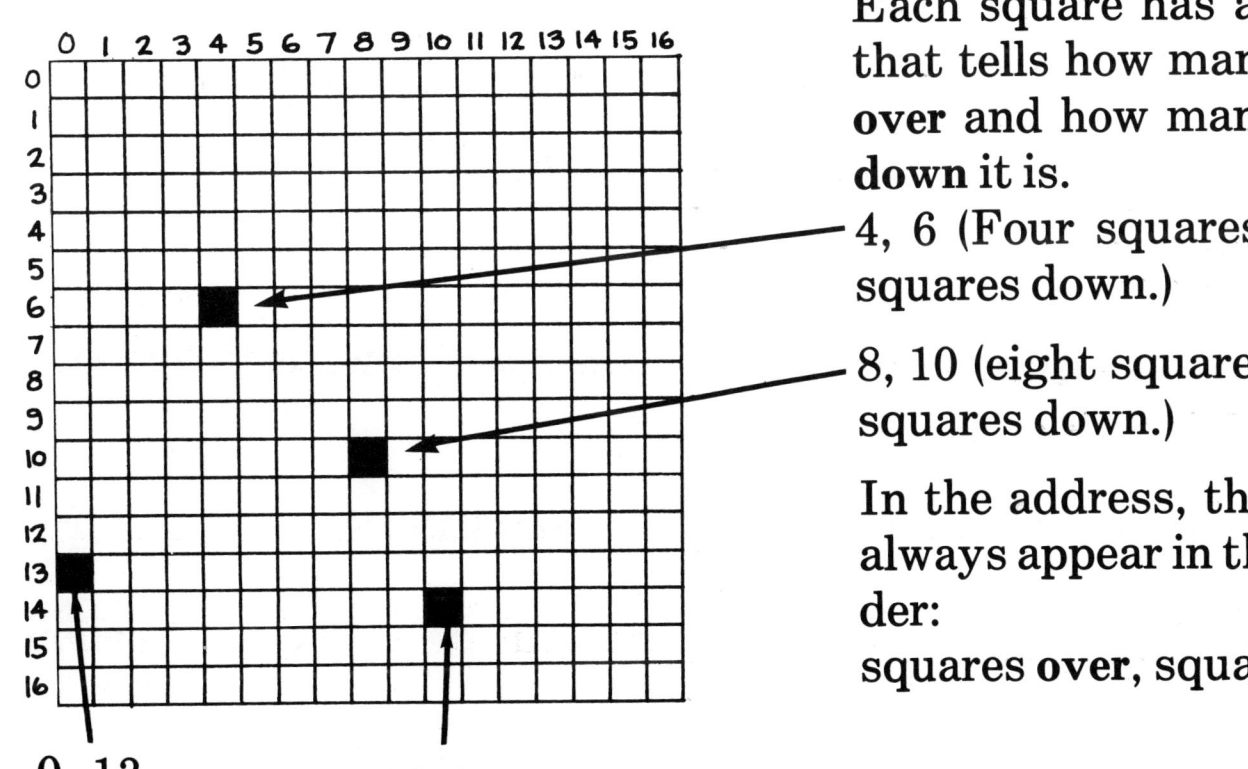

Each square has an address that tells how many squares **over** and how many squares **down** it is.

4, 6 (Four squares over, six squares down.)

8, 10 (eight squares over, six squares down.)

In the address, the numbers always appear in the same order:

squares **over**, squares **down**

To light up a square, you use **PLOT**.

```
 5  GR
10  COLOR=12
15  PLOT 8,12
20  PLOT 13,7
25  PLOT 11,16
```

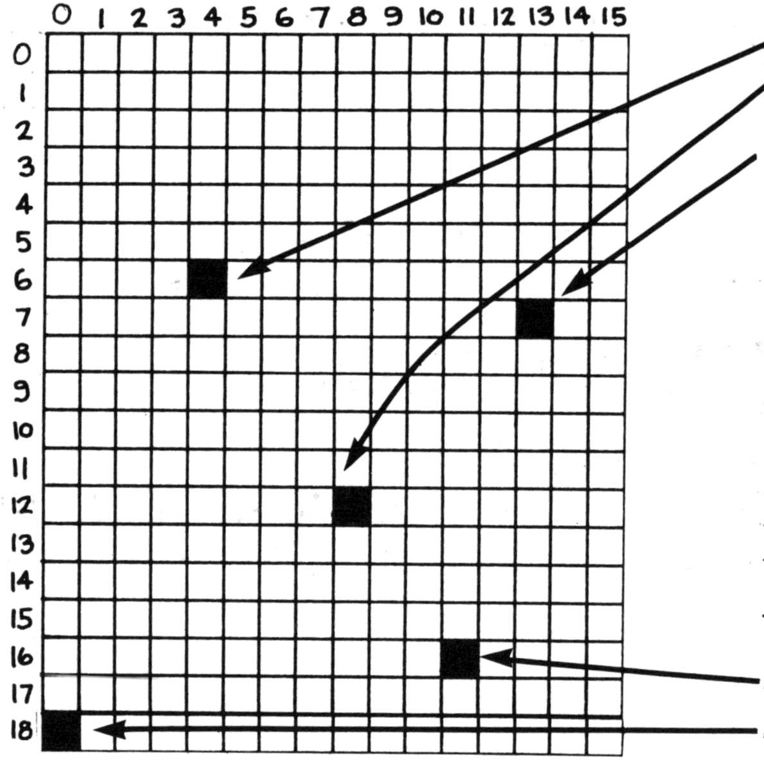

Let's put some more PLOT statements in this program, but first let's change the color:

```
30  COLOR=11
```

Now, anything we PLOT after line 30 will be pink, unless we change colors again!

```
35  PLOT 4,6
40  PLOT 0,18
45  END
```

Every time you begin a graphics program with

```
 5  GR
```

you are really doing *two* things at once:

1. Telling the computer you will be drawing a picture on most of the screen.

2. Setting the color to zero. This means that if you forget to put a COLOR statement in your program, every square you PLOT will automatically be color zero, which is black. Since the background color is also black, you won't be able to see what you are drawing!

Be careful you don't forget to choose a color for your graphics programs!

If you want to light up a line across the screen, you would have to use many PLOT statements.

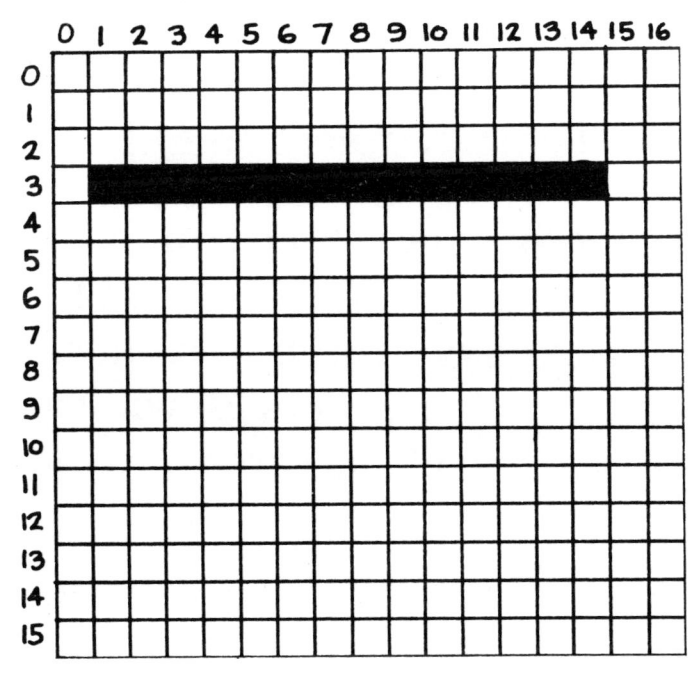

```
5   GR
10  COLOR=6
15  PLOT 1,3
20  PLOT 2,3
25  PLOT 3,3
30  PLOT 4,3
35  PLOT 5,3
40  PLOT 6,3
45  PLOT 7,3
50  PLOT 8,3
```

and so on.

For a program that would fill most of the screen, you would be up all night, typing in PLOT statements!

BUT—there is an easier way to do the same thing.

HLIN will help us write the same program much more easily:

```
5  GR
10 COLOR=6
15 HLIN 1,14 AT 3
20 END
```

HLIN 1, 14 at 3 tells the computer to light up the squares across the screen from 1 to 14 (start at 1 and end at 14). It also says the line should be "at 3" squares **down** from the top of the screen.

HLIN is short for "horizontal line."

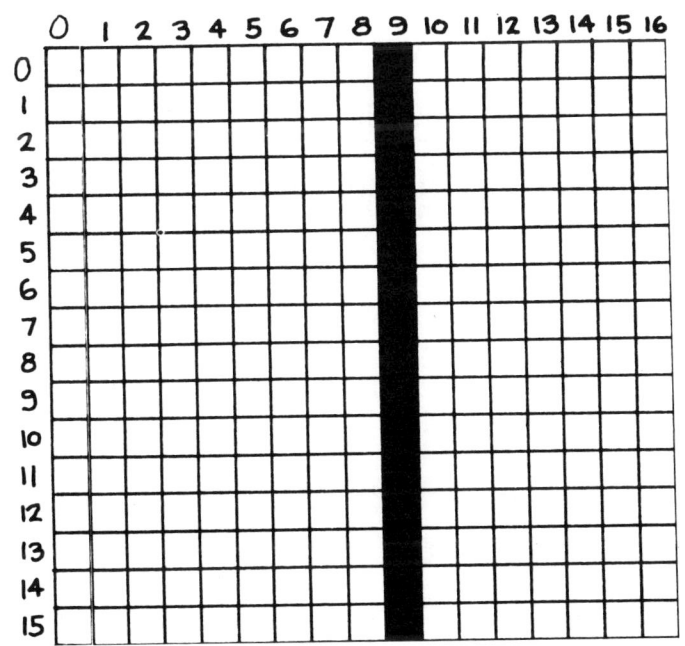

To light up a line going up and down the screen, we use
VLIN
which stands for "vertical line".

```
5  GR
10 COLOR=8
15 VLIN 0,15 AT 9
20 END
```

This lights up the squares up and down the screen, beginning at 0 and ending at 15. This line will be "at 9" squares **across** the screen.

VLIN and HLIN make graphics programs *very* easy! By using PLOT, VLIN, HLIN, and lots of color changes, you can make a picture of anything you like!

Just for fun, you might want to make your picture **blink** off and on. You will need a GOTO statement in your program to do this.

Remember that when the computer comes to a GR statement when it is executing your program, it automatically makes the color equal to zero (black). This makes it look like your picture has disappeared, because you can't see a black picture against a black background.

Let's use this information to make a "blinking line" program.

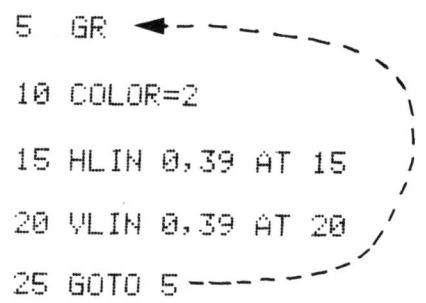

```
5  GR
10 COLOR=2
15 HLIN 0,39 AT 15
20 VLIN 0,39 AT 20
25 GOTO 5
```

After your two dark blue lines are lighted up, line 25 makes the computer go back to 5 and start over by making the screen black. This makes your lines blink on and off!

For your first graphics program, you might want to make your initials on the screen. You could make each initial a different color, or you could have them blink on and off.

When you plan your graphics programs, you will find it very helpful to use graph paper. Remember that there are 40 squares across and 40 squares down on the graphics screen, but they are numbered from **zero** to **39**. If you try to use addresses with numbers bigger than 39, you will get an error message when you run the program: ILLEGAL QUANTITY ERROR

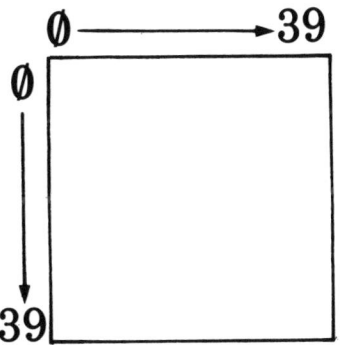

When you write a long graphics program, you will need more than those four lines under the graphics screen to LIST your program and look it over before you RUN it.

If you switch back to TEXT *before* you type LIST, the computer can list the program on the whole screen. You might forget to do this the first few times, but once you get used to it, writing graphics programs will be easier to do.

SECTION 11: Sample Programs

COMPUTER PANIC

```
5   TEXT
10  HOME
15  PRINT "HELP!  THIS COMPUTER IS CRAZY!"
20  GOTO 10
```

GUESSING FUN

```
5   TEXT
10  HOME
15  PRINT "PICK A NUMBER.  TYPE IT IN"
20  PRINT "THE CHOICES ARE 1, 2, OR 3"
25  INPUT N
30  IF N=1 THEN PRINT "YOU WILL BE RICH."
35  IF N=2 THEN PRINT "YOU WILL BE FAMOUS."
40  IF N=3 THEN PRINT "YOU WILL HAVE 13 CHILDREN."
45  END
```

PINE TREE

```
 5  TEXT
 8  HOME
10  PRINT "      X"
15  PRINT "     XXX"
20  PRINT "    XXXXX"
25  PRINT "   XXXXXXX"
30  PRINT "  XXXXXXXXX"
35  PRINT "XXXXXXXXXXX"
40  PRINT "     X"
45  PRINT "     X"
50  PRINT "     X"
55  END
```

make sure you skip enough spaces in each line!

COLORING THE SCREEN

```
 5  GR
10  COLOR=6
15  FOR Z=0 TO 39
20  HLIN 0,39 AT Z
25  NEXT Z
30  END
```

ARITHMETIC

```
 5  TEXT              35  PRINT "A+B="
10  HOME              40  PRINT  A+B
15  LET A=1           45  PRINT
20  LET B=2           50  PRINT "C*D="
25  LET C=3           55  PRINT C*D
30  LET D=4           60  END
```

SECTION 12: Glossary of Statements and Commands

CATALOG—tells the computer to turn on the disk drive, and print out a list of the names of programs stored on that diskette.

COLOR—tells the computer your color choice for a graphics program. The colors are numbered from 0 to 15. For example, to choose the color yellow:

$$35\ COLOR = 13$$

CONT—continues the execution of a program after you have stopped it by using $\boxed{CTRL}$ — $\boxed{C}$.

$\boxed{CTRL}$—$\boxed{C}$—stops the execution of a program and prints out the line number where the program stopped running.

DELETE—erases a program from the diskette. For example, to erase JOHN'S PROGRAM from the diskette:

$$DELETE\ JOHN'S\ PROGRAM$$

END—tells the computer the program is over.

FOR-NEXT—a type of do-loop which has the computer perform some action a certain number of times.

        Example: 10 FOR X = 1 TO 100
                         15 PRINT "HELLO"
                         20 NEXT X

GOTO—tells the computer to skip to a certain line number in the program.

GR—reserves the top part of the screen for graphics, and automatically sets the color to zero, which is black.

HLIN—used in graphics programs to light up a horizontal line on the screen.

        Example: HLIN 0, 39 AT 15 lights up a line across the screen from 0 to 39, at 15 squares down the screen.

HOME— In a TEXT program, HOME clears everything off the screen and returns the cursor to the top left corner.

In a graphics program, HOME clears the four lines on the bottom of the screen which are used for typing, and returns the cursor to just below the graphics part of the screen.

IF-THEN—a type of branch statement which puts a "test" in the program. If the test is passed, the computer must follow special directions. If the test is not passed, the computer will drop down to the next line in the program.

INPUT—types out a question mark when the program is executed, and waits for an answer to be typed in. The answer is stored in a certain memory space.
>			Example: 15 PRINT "TYPE IN YOUR AGE."
>			20 INPUT N

In this example, the answer is stored in mailbox N.

LET—assigns a number to a memory space (or variable)
>			Example: 15 LET R = 96

LIST—prints out a list, in order, of the program statements you have typed into the memory.

LOAD—loads a program from a cassette tape into the computer's memory.

JACK'S PROGRAM—loads a program (this one named LOAD JACK'S PROGRAM) from the diskette into the computer's memory.

NEW—erases the old program from the memory.

PLOT—In a graphics program, PLOT lights up the square of light at the address you choose.
                Example: 35 PLOT 5, 19
lights up the square at 5 times over and 19 squares down on the TV screen.

PRINT—tells the computer you want it to write something on the screen.

$\boxed{\text{RESET}}$—immediately stops the execution of your program, but does not erase it from the memory. After you push $\boxed{\text{RESET}}$, you will have to start all over if you want to RUN your program again. Use $\boxed{\text{RESET}}$ if you just don't know what else to do, but you don't want to erase your program by turning off the keyboard. (You will use $\boxed{\text{RESET}}$ if you goof while loading or saving a cassette tape.)

RETURN—you must press this key each time you finish typing in a line.

RUN—starts the execution of the program. This command is *not* part of the program itself, and does not have a line number.

SAVE—records your program on a cassette tape. (This does *not* erase your program from the memory. Only NEW, or turning off the keyboard, will do that.)

SAVE DANNY'S INITIAL PROGRAM—records the program from the memory (this program is named DANNY'S INITIAL PROGRAM) onto a diskette. (This does *not* erase your program from the memory. Only NEW, or turning off the keyboard, will do that.)

TEXT—reserves the entire TV screen for writing letters or numbers (rather than drawing pictures).

VLIN—used in graphics programs to light up a vertical line on the screen.
      Example: 85 VLIN 0, 39 AT 12

lights up a line up and down the screen from 0 to 39, at 12 squares over on the screen.

NAME _____

Simulate these computer runs. Show your "printout" on the screen.

```
10 CLS
20 PRINT "BIG"
30 PRINT
40 PRINT "YELLOW"
50 PRINT "BLUE"
60 END
```

```
10 CLS
20 PRINT "THE ANSWER"
30 PRINT 30 * 2
40 PRINT 30 + 2
50 PRINT 30 - 2
60 PRINT "THE END"
70 END
```

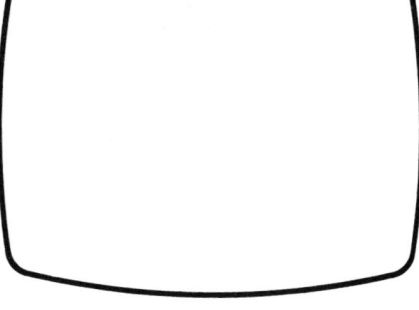

NAME _____

Here is a program and "printout." Find and fix the mistakes in the programs so a run will produce what is shown on the screen.

```
10 CLS
20 PRINT 20 + 6
30 PRINT 30 + 4
35 PRINT
40 PRINT "60 - 3"
50 PRINT 10 - 10
60 PRINT "HELLO"
70 END
```

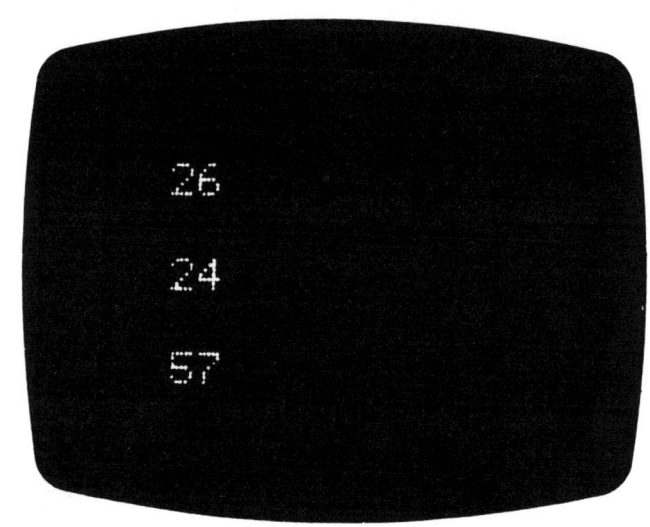

NAME _____

Write the program to print out the pattern shown below. Make the hair yellow, the eyes blue, the mouth red, and the shirt green. Don't forget the END statement.

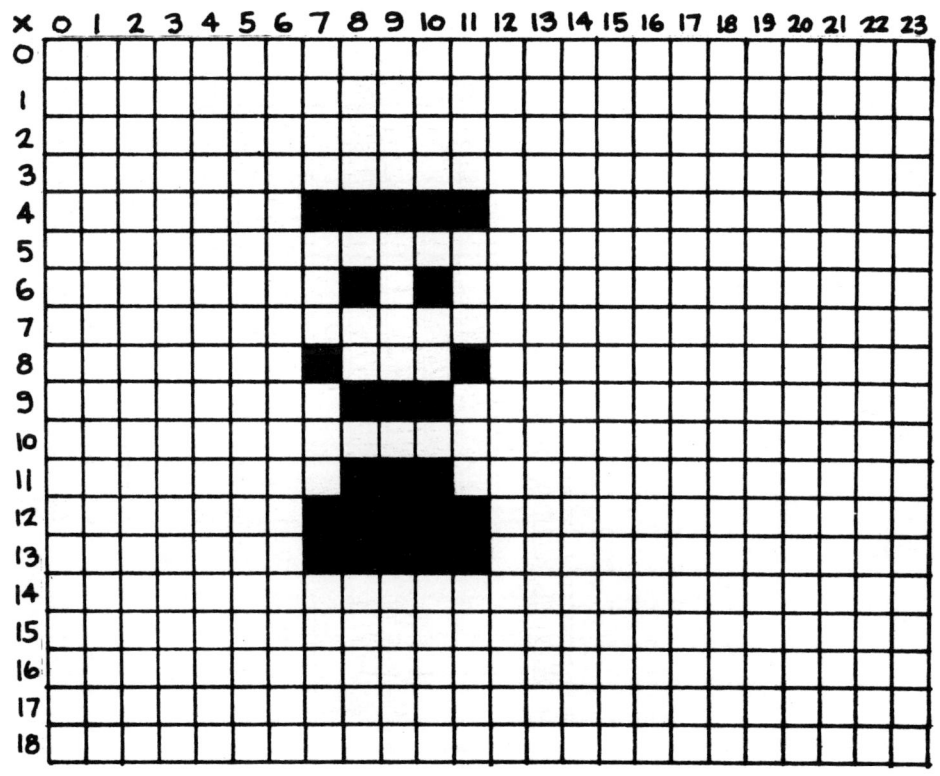

NAME _____

On the graph below, color in each dot which will light up when you run this program. Use crayons or colored pencils to show the correct color.

```
5  GR. 0
10 COLOR = 8
15 PLOT 5,5
20 PLOT 6,4
25 PLOT 6,5
30 COLOR = 13
35 FOR P = 1 TO 10
40 PLOT 3,P
45 NEXT P
50 COLOR = 9
55 PLOT 18,18
60 PLOT 0,0
65 PLOT 15,0
70 PLOT 0,15
75 END
```

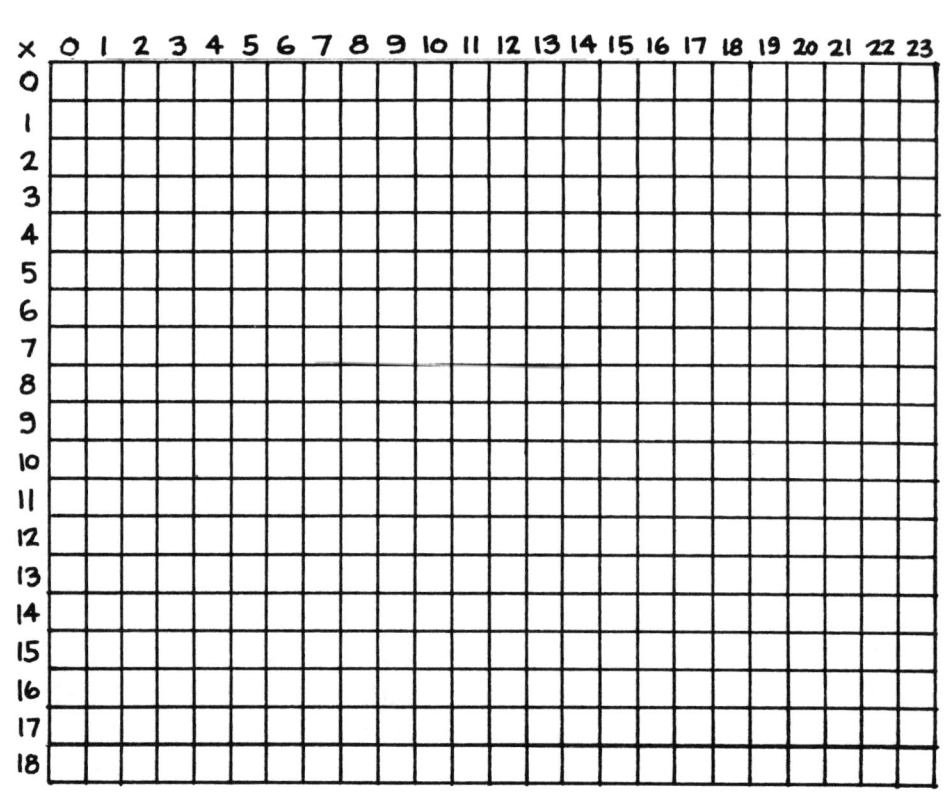

Notes for Teachers and Parents

I am not, by any stretch of the imagination, a sophisticated programmer. I took one programming course in college, and have spent the past four years working with elementary school children. I've taught microcomputer programming to nearly 300 children, ranging in age from 4 to 12, and have yet to run into any children who aren't dying to get their hands on the keyboard. Computers are a *natural*—they give immediate feedback, and allow children to create something all their own. I love teaching programming. It is one of the most exciting things I've ever done.

Candidates for teaching programming to young children must have one trait above all others—the ability to interact with the children on a peer level, and learn along *with* them. Computer programming is not just a skill—it is a *tool*. You learn programming not as a study in itself, but because of what you can accomplish with it. In any one computer program, there are many ways to approach and solve the problem at hand. The thing I say most often to my students is, "Run it, and see if it works!"

I won't presume to tell you just now to go about teaching your particular group of children, but I would like to share some of my successful ideas, and some of my failures. These are the things which have worked, or not worked, with every group of children I've taught in the past few years.

One word from someone who's been there: book some computer time for yourself during each week, before you start teaching the children. Once they've had a few lessons, they'll insist you stand in line like everyone else!

General Hints

If you have had no previous experience with the APPLE II PLUS, before you do anything else, read through the manuals which come with the machine. (At the time this book went to press, several manuals, some better than others, were available for the novice programmer.) It is especially important to understand the directions for setting up the machine, and the safety precautions. To gain an overview of this book, you may wish to read through the children's portion before you work through the APPLE II PLUS manuals. It will not be necessary to learn everything in the manuals—check the glossary of this book for the most crucial statements and commands.

This book is designed to accompany the APPLE II PLUS machine, which has APPLESOFT built into the computer. Because of the relatively large number of directions concerned with operating this particular model of the APPLE computer line, it would be possible, but impractical, to use this text with another model. Such use would require considerable adaptation on your part before a child could use the text effectively.

Refer to your manuals for complete instructions on maintaining your computer, but these seem to be the most common pitfalls:

1. If you move the computer around from place to place, it is necessary to open the cover and check to see that the cards (if any) are firmly seated in the slots *before* you turn on the computer. If they have worked loose in transit, you could ruin a card.
2. The three-pronged plug is not just a nicety. The computer must be grounded for it to function properly. Don't bypass the function of the grounded plug by using an adaptor without a ground wire.
3. The cords and wires coming from the back of your computer must be protected from being accidentally jerked out. Make sure you have located the computer in a place where the cords are protected from falling objects, feet, and contending programmers.
4. Have a clear understanding as to which people have the responsibility for opening the cover and working with the hardware inside the computer. (Too many cooks make sauce out of the APPLE.)

SETTING UP YOUR COMPUTER CENTER: Since programmers tend to get excited and vocal, I suggest that you locate your computer in a semi-secluded area which is near someone in your school who understands the machine. If the children have any problems with the computer, they are going to come and find you anyway, and it's easier if they don't have to call you down the hall from another room.

Secure the electrical cords in a way that keeps them out of the traffic pattern around the computer. Stepping on the cords may cause a fire hazard and will create fuzz on the TV screen.

I schedule only two children at the computer during one time slot. They usually help each other if they encounter difficulties. More than two children at one time may encourage fighting over who will do the typing.

Have enough room for several chairs around the keyboard, and consider where you will place the computer when you teach a group. Sometimes I have used a kitchen timer to keep the children moving, and other times I have run the schedule by the clock. It depends on your group. You will keep your sanity longer if you enforce the rule: "When your turn is over, it's OVER."

A computer notebook for each child is a must. They should learn to take notes on how to do things, or they will never become confident programmers. Discourage them from running to you for answers they should have in their notes.

You may wonder why I have so few sample programs in this book. I have found that the more timid programmers will never pull away from the safety of typing in *my* programs every time they are on the machine, unless I provide very vew samples, and force them to think up their own.

It sounds, from the tone of these hints, that I have many problems with children who program. That isn't the case at all. However, a seemingly trivial problem can eat up precious time when 50 children are waiting to use one computer.

The most important thing you as the teacher must do is to give the children an *overall* view of the problem you are trying to program. They must see that a problem can be broken down into sections, and then each section can be accomplished on the computer in several different ways. Teaching only *what* a statement does, without focusing on *why* you would want to use it, creates frustrations for most children.

My biggest failure of all time . . . I can't emphasize this one enough. Don't ever let your children play commercial game tapes until they are accomplished programmers! By 'accomplished,' I mean the end of the first year for most children.

Let's face it—playing 'Breakout' or 'Computer Hockey' is much more fun, and a lot less work, than learning to program. Especially for elementary school children. If they discover that they can play game tapes on the school computer, they will lose all interest in doing the work involved in learning to program. This is a sad but true fact, and one I learned the *hard* way. Even with your 12-year-olds, you will regret the day you ever brought a game tape into your computer center. Overnight, they will change from being thrilled about having the chance to try their own programs, to being disappointed because their favorite game tape has been retired. Certainly, they'll have a chance to play games on the computer. But the games should be those that *they* have written themselves.

GROUP INSTRUCTION: Choose for your computer center a room which has effective shades on the windows. When I teach a group, I place the TV facing them, and I sit at an angle to the keyboard. We talk over what we want to accomplish, and I do the typing. Unless you have a crackerjack typist in the group, it makes lessons unbearably slow if the whole class has to wait while someone hunts and pecks on the keys.

Suggested Lesson Outline - Once a Week Lessons

Do not go on to the next topic until all the children have had a chance to try out their last lesson on the computer, or they will never remember it. A weekly schedule is imperative for assuring individual children their time at the computer. With the exception of SAVE and LOAD, these lessons follow the sequence of the book.

SECTION 1
   1. What is a computer?

SECTION 2
   2. Introduce flowcharting

3. Practice writing flowcharts
4. More practice on flowcharts

SECTION 3

5. Using the keyboard, running the machine itself, behavior guidelines, scheduling, RETURN

SECTION 6

6. Beginning programming: HOME, TEXT, CTRL-S, CTRL-C, CONT, NEW, LIST, RUN with PRINT examples

SECTION 7

7. PRINT statements with quotation marks, SYNTAX ERROR, TEXT and HOME in programs
8. PRINT to skip lines; editing
9. PRINT with arithmetic operations (+, −, *, /)
10. PRINT variables—simple
11. PRINT variables such as PRINT A + B

SECTION 4 or 5

12. Operation of disk drive *or* cassette recorder

SECTION 8

13. GOTO
14. INPUT

SECTION 9

15. FOR-NEXT with PRINT and arithmetic statements
16. More work on FOR-NEXT
17. IF-THEN test
18. IF-THEN in more complex programs (draw flowchart of program function)

SECTION 10

19. Discussion of PLOT, COLOR, and plotting of coordinates on paper
20. Graphics worksheets
21. Graphics—make their own initials with PLOT
22. Graphics—HLIN and VLIN
23. Blinking graphics; more complex programs, such as filling the screen with a color

SECTION 11

24. Discuss possibilities for designing and carrying out their own programs

Teaching Suggestions For Each Section

Section 1: What is a computer?

Comparisons to home computer games are helpful. Most children think computers are 'smart', and younger children will think they are 'magic'. Don't overexplain—make arrangements to get the children at the machine as soon as feasible. None of your explanations will really make sense until then. You might want to write a simple INPUT program they can use for some 'hands-on' practice.

Section 2: Flowcharting

The objective is logical thinking, not perfection. Have fun! Choose 'How To' type topics, which have built-in choices. They must be about something the children understand.

> How to: Give the dog a bath; Make pizza; Build a doghouse; Lose your allowance; Make a phone call to Grandma

Set a minimum number of do-loops or branches. I usually set a minimum of three. Use manilla drawing paper. Have the children write the words first, *then* draw the boxes around the words. It's easier!

Section 3: Running the machine itself

Be careful to use the words 'save' and 'load' properly, when you talk about the disk drive or cassette recorder, or the children will confuse the two terms. Typing practice on school typewriters or those at home will help the children accomplish much more during their turn at the computer. Children who practice on manual typewriters tend to *pound* on the computer keys. This will cause typing errors and other keyboard problems.

Section 4: Saving your programs with a cassette recorder

The cassette player system for saving programs is a headache for many people, but it is my opinion that they have trouble because they do one of these things incorrectly:

a. They use poor quality recording tape, or try to save programs over old recordings.
b. They use a more expensive tape recorder, which not only records the signals from the computer, but picks up background noise from the tape as well. In this case, more is not better.
c. They don't leave enough space on the tape between programs.
d. They don't teach the children how to use the counter properly.
e. They continually fiddle with the volume controls. Find the best settings for your machine, and then tape the volume controls shut, so no one can change them. (If you are loading tapes made on another machine, or from a commercial source, you *will* have to adjust the volume and tone controls to make them load properly.)
f. They don't save one program twice on the same tape, to insure that at least one of them will turn out.

Section 5: Saving your programs with a disk drive

You should record on one side of the diskette only. When you put the diskette into the disk drive, the label goes *up*.

Static electricity will ruin the disk drive. Stress to the children that they must ground-themselves-out each time they touch the disk drive, especially if you have carpeting in the school, or if the diskette is cold. This is done by touching the power source, next to the ON-OFF switch.

When moving the disk drive in its packing box, tape the door shut. If you catch the door on the packing material, it will snap off.

Section 6: Getting ready to program

Written quizzes on the meaning of the commands and statements accomplish very little. Let the children learn about this while they type in their own programs. If they don't know what they're doing, their program simply won't run.

Teach the difference between *commands* and *statements*. If they do not understand this difference, the children will be frustrated the first few times they work at the computer. Typically, they will type in a program without any line numbers, and then will not be able to understand why none of the program is in the memory to be listed later.

Section 7: PRINT and variables

At the back of the book, you will find samples of PRINT worksheets. This is one of the few areas in which worksheets are of real value.

Discourage the children from using the letter 'O' as a variable. It tends to be confusing.

I use only variables of one letter with beginning programmers. They may get confused, using word-length variables which look to them like statements.

Using TEXT and HOME at the beginning of each program, even though it may seem rather cumbersome at first, will prevent a great many problems that can arise when many people use the same computer.

Section 8: GOTO and INPUT

Every PRINT line moves the cursor down to the next line. This problem will come up when you teach FOR-NEXT loops with several PRINT statements in the middle.

Look up the use of the semi-colon in the APPLE II PLUS manuals. Sooner or later, someone will ask you how to make things PRINT right next to each other on the same line when using several PRINT statements.

Section 9: IF-THEN and FOR-NEXT

Reminder: variables must match on FOR-NEXT loops.

The children will have trouble remembering that the computer drops down to the next line if the test is not met in an IF-THEN statement.

Flowcharts may be helpful in tracing the functions of loops and branches in more complex programs. Don't be overly concerned with detail when you draw them.

'X is not equal to Y' is written as $X <> Y$ or $X >< Y$.

Section 10: Graphics programs

The 'over and down' motion of plotting a graphics point on the coordinates is similar to drawing a large '7' on the screen.

I have included sample worksheets for practicing coordinates in the back of this book. This is very helpful, especially for the younger students.

When the children number the squares of their graph paper, have them put an 'X' in the upper left-hand corner square. This helps prevent mistakes in numbering.

X	0	1	2	3	4	5	6
0							
1							
2							
3							

Tracing the 'Numbers' program through its memory changes is helpful for showing how the values of variables change in a program. (This program may be found at the end of Section 9.)

Use crayons or markers to plan graphics pictures in the actual colors you will use.

Section 11: Sample programs

As stated earlier, with the more timid programmers, I find that too many examples inhibit experimentation.

If you are using a cassette recorder, all the children should have their own cassette for saving their programs. Buying some gummed labels is a good investment, so that they will not have trouble trying to locate those programs at a later date.

Go through your diskettes periodically and delete those programs which have been updated, or are no longer being used.

Section 12: Glossary

For those examples in which I used statements, as opposed to commands, I put line numbers in front of each program line, to help remind the children.

Student, Meet Computer. Creative Computing Makes the Introduction

Free Catalogs

Three new catalogs are available **free**. The **Fall 1980 Creative Computing Press Catalog** features the full line of Creative Computing books and merchandise. The **Sensational Software Catalog** describes 150 software packages for eleven popular computers. The **Creative Computing Catalog** includes the best books from other publishers.

Make the most of your computer resources. Write for all three free catalogs today!

Blank Cassettes

The quality of cassette tape used to save and load programs is an important factor in getting the programs to run. Tape quality for computers is measured differently from quality for audio tape. The tape must be capable of sending to the computer the electronic signals of the program without transmitting extraneous noises that could interfere with the ability of the computer to load the tape.

Our blank cassettes are tested and recommended for computer use. C-10 cassette, 5 min. per side, blank label on each side in a Norelco hard plastic box. [0010] $1.25 each.

Computer Coin Games

GRADES 7 AND UP

Play "Tic Tac Toe," "Guess a Word," "Create a Pattern" and "Escape the Network." This book is an ideal introduction to the complicated concepts of computer circuitry.

Games Magazine says "Whether or not you have any experience with computer technology you'll be both amazed and delighted by the simplicity of the format and the complexity of the play. All you need is some common cents."

Dr. Dobb's Journal says **Computer Coin Games** is a simple approach to a complicated concept...**Computer Coin Games** is liberally sprinkled with clever illustrations and diagrams, and provides a relatively painless route to an understanding of how computer circuits function."

Written by Joe Weisbecker and enhanced with great cartoons by Sunstone Graphics. 96 pages, paperbound, (10R) $3.95

Joe Weisbecker

Learning how computer circuitry works can actually be fun. All you have to do is slide around a few pennies. Computer Coin Games presents a series of interesting games with full size playing boards that trace the paths of electronic signals through various simple computer circuits.

Beginning with the "basic penny switch flip flop" the games build in difficulty until the reader is creating intricate networks. Why binary math is used in computers and how it works, how the computer counts, adds, subtracts, uses a number base, and handles letters and words, are all explained in the book.

Problems for Computer Solution

GRADE 9 AND UP

Stephen J. Rogowski

90 intriguing and fascinating problems, each thoroughly discussed and referenced, make an excellent source of exercises in research and problem solving. Arithmetic, algebra, geometry, number theory, probability and science are examples of the 11 types of problems included. The book contains 7 appendices and 3 classic unsolved problems.

Dr. Dobb's Journal says "The problems are clearly and concisely stated."

The great classroom book is 104 pp. 8½ x 11" Softbound. (9Z) $4.95.

The Teacher Edition contains solutions to the problems, each with a complete listing in BASIC, sample run, and an in-depth analysis explaining the algorithms and theory involved. It is 192 pp. 8½ x 11" Softbound. (9Y) $9.95

Be A Computer Literate

GRADES 4 TO 8

Marion J. Ball and Sylvia Charp

This informative, full color book is an ideal first introduction to the world of computers. Covers kinds of computers, how they work, their applications in society, flowcharts and writing a simple program. Full color drawings, diagrams and photos on every page coupled with large type make this book easy to read and understand. Used as a text in many schools. 66 pp softbound, $3.95 (6H).

GRADE 4 AND UP
Basic Computer Games

Edited by David H. Ahl, this is a complete anthology of 101 favorite games and simulations, each complete with sample run, program listing, and description. All games run in standard Microsoft Basic with a Basic conversion table included. Easy to run with any computer. The imaginative and challenging games are for one, two, or more players. Play Basketball, Craps, Gomoko, Blackjack, Even Wins, Super Star Trek, Bombs Away, Horserace. Simulate lunar landings. Play the stock market. Write poetry. Draw pictures. 125,000 copies in print. 192 pp. 8½ x 11" softbound. (6C) $7.50.

More Basic Computer Games

Edited by David H. Ahl and Steve North, this fantastic sequel to Basic Computer Games contains sample run, program listing and description for 84 new games. All games run in standard Microsoft Basic and a Basic conversion table is included. Dr. Dobb's says, "Whether you are interested in war games, gambling, sports, grids and mazes, space, psychology, drag racing or throwing mudballs, More Basic Computer Games has something in it for you." Evade a man-eating rabbit, crack a safe, tame a wild horse, become a millionaire, race your Ferrari, joust with a knight, trek across the desert on your camel, navigate in deep space. 200 pp. 8½ x 11" softbound. (6C2) $7.95.

TRS-80 Edition

Edited by David Ahl and Steve North, all 84 games are converted to run on Level II 16K TRS-80 machines. Radio Shack users will delight that the conversion work on these imaginative and challenging games has been done for them. Just type the listing in to your machine for endless hours of fun. 200 pp. 8½ x 11" softbound. (6C4) $7.95.

GRADES 3 TO 8
Computer Rage

Computer Rage has been hailed by educators as an outstanding game for teaching youngsters between 7 and 14 about the binary number system (the game uses 3 binary dice!), parts of a computer system and how a program is processed. In addition the game is sheer fun! Recommended by Instructor,, The Arithmetic Teacher, The Science Teacher, Curriculum Product Review and others.

Computer Rage is based on a large scale multiprocessing computer system. The objective is to move your three programs from input to output. Moves are determined by the roll of three binary dice representing bits in a computer. Hazards include priority interrupts, program bugs, decision symbols, power failures and restricted input and output channels. Notes are included for adapting game for school instruction. A perfect introductory tool to binary math and the seemingly-complex computer. $8.95 (6Z)

Binary Dice. Now, the same dice used in Computer Rage can be purchased separately. Three binary dice (red, green and blue) in ziplock bag. $1.25 (3G)

ALL GRADE LEVELS
Computers in Mathematics: A Sourcebook of Ideas

Edited by David Ahl

Here is a huge sourcebook of ideas for using computers in mathematics instruction. This large format book contains sections on computer literacy, problem solving techniques, art and graphing, simulations, computer assisted instruction, probability, functions, magic squares and programming styles.

One section presents over 250 problems, puzzles and programming ideas--more than is found in most "collection of problems" books.

Pragmatic, ready-to-use, classroom tested ideas are presented for everything from the most basic introduction to binary numbers to advanced techniques like multiple regression analysis and differential equations. Every item discussed has a complete explanation including flowcharts, programs and sample runs.

Much of the material has appeared in **Creative Computing** but the back issues are no longer available. Hence this is your only source to this practical and valuable material. Edited by David H. Ahl, this mammoth 224-page softbound book costs only $15.95. (The individual issues, if they were available, would cost over $60.00). [12D]

GRADES K TO 4
Katie and the Computer

Fred D'Ignazio and Stan Gilliam have created a delightful picture book adventure that explains to a child how a computer works. Katie "falls" into the imaginary land of Cybernia inside her Daddy's home computer. In her journey she meets the Software Colonel, the Bytes, the Table Manager, and even a ferocious Program Bug. Her journey parallels the path of a simple command through the stages of processing in a computer, which introduces the fundamentals of computer operation to 4 to 10 year olds. Supplemental explanatory information on computers, bytes, hardware and software is contained in the front and back end papers. 42 pp. 11 x 8½" casebound. (12A) $6.95.

To Order

Send your check for books plus $2.00 shipping and handling per order to Creative Computing, P.O. Box 789-M, Morristown, NJ 07960. NJ residents add 5% sales tax. Visa, Master Charge or American Express are also acceptable. For faster service, call in your bank card order toll free to

800-631-8112
(in NJ, call 201-540-0445)

creative computing

P.O. Box 789-M, Morristown, NJ 07960

Notes

Notes

Notes

Notes